© 1989 Franklin Watts

First published in Great Britain
    1989 by
Franklin Watts
12a Golden Square
London W1R 4BA

First published in the USA by
Franklin Watts Inc
387 Park Avenue South
New York
NY 10016

First published in Australia by
Franklin Watts
14 Mars Road
Lane Cove
NSW 2066

UK ISBN: 0 86313 849 7
US ISBN: 0-531-10726-4
Library of Congress Catalog
Card Number: 88-36284

**Series Editor**
Norman Barrett

**Designed by**
Edward Kinsey

**Photographs by**
Aerospatiale
Agusta Group
Bell Helicopter Textron
Boeing Vertol Company
BP Oil
Bristow Helicopters
British International Helicopters
Civil Aviation Authority
MBB
NATO
Shell
Westland Helicopters

**Technical Consultant**
J. M. G. Gradidge

# The Picture World of
# Helicopters

## CONTENTS

| | |
|---|---|
| Introduction | 6 |
| Flying a helicopter | 8 |
| Types of helicopters | 10 |
| Carrying and lifting | 12 |
| Carrying people | 14 |
| Special operations | 16 |
| Fighting helicopters | 23 |
| Facts | 26 |
| Glossary | 28 |
| Index | 29 |

# Introduction

Helicopters are flying machines that can take off and land straight up and down. They can hover, or stay in one spot in the air.

Unlike aeroplanes, helicopters do not need a runway. They have rotors instead of wings. The rotors whirl around. They are moving wings.

▽ The quickest way to get around a crowded city is by helicopter. Helicopters have many uses. They can do things that aeroplanes cannot do.

▷ Helicopters are able to fly slowly and to hover, or stay in one spot in the air. This makes them ideal for such tasks as rescue and observation work and lifting people or things.

▽ Helicopters on a riverside heliport. A heliport is an airport for helicopters. But unlike an airport, it takes up very little space. As a result, helicopters can operate from the heart of a busy city.

# Flying a helicopter

Flying a helicopter is more difficult than flying an ordinary aeroplane. Helicopters can fly backwards and sideways, as well as hover. The pilot must be able to handle several controls at once.

△ A helicopter hovers as the pilot prepares to land. This looks like a simple manoeuvre, but it calls for special skills.

△ A helicopter
cockpit, with two sets
of controls. The second
set is for the co-pilot.
The foot pedals control
the direction of the
helicopter. At the side
of the seats are hand
controls for speed. The
pilot uses the curved
levers to move the
helicopter's nose up
and down.

◁ The pilot in his
cockpit.

# Types of helicopters

Helicopters are made in different sizes, depending on their use. Most types have one main rotor, with a smaller one at the tail.

   Some helicopters have two large rotors, to provide more lifting power. They turn in opposite directions so that the helicopter does not spin.

▽ A Puma helicopter, with a powerful main rotor and a small tail rotor to keep the machine from spinning.

△ A Boeing Vertol Chinook has two main rotors. They spin in opposite directions.

▷ A helicopter fitted with "skids" instead of landing wheels. Skids enable a helicopter to land on uneven ground. They stop it rolling.

# Carrying and lifting

Helicopters are able to carry a limited amount of cargo. They need more power than an aeroplane to carry the same weight.

But they are ideal vehicles for lifting and positioning heavy pieces of equipment. Some, called flying cranes, are specially designed for this purpose.

△ Loading baggage into the hold of a Boeing Vertol. This is one of the largest passenger helicopters. It can carry more than 40 people.

▷ A Boeing Vertol Chinook, adapted as a flying crane, lowers a heavy piece of equipment into place.

# Carrying people

Different passenger helicopters carry anything from two to fifty people. They are a fast means of transporting people over short distances.

They are also used to take people over difficult land or sea routes. They can land workers on offshore oil rigs and carry doctors and nurses to places hard to reach by other means.

▽ Helicopters are used as feeder transport to airports. Passengers can be picked up at heliports in cities or business people can be flown from their offices direct to an airport.

△ Former President, Ronald Reagan, is met as he steps off from a helicopter. Time is important for such people as politicians and top executives. They regularly use helicopters as a speedy means of transport.

▷ The average passenger helicopter carries between 10 and 30 people.

# Special operations

The helicopter is used by police, fire-fighting and rescue services. It can reach places where other vehicles cannot go. It provides a bird's-eye view of what is going on down below. This makes it useful in search operations, whether for criminals or for people in trouble.

△ The police use helicopters in town and in the country. They can be used to track cars or to patrol places unreachable by other means of transport. They are often used to report on how traffic is moving on the roads below.

▷ A fireman is winched down from a helicopter. The fire services use helicopters for rescue work from rooftops and other high places.

▽ A helicopter drops special chemicals to put out a bush fire. Fire-fighting helicopters are used in wooded country to get to the heart of a fire.

An important use for helicopters is the saving of lives. They are used by the coastguard in search and rescue operations. People in trouble on the seas or stranded by the tide can be winched to safety.

Helicopters also play a part in medical services. They can carry vital medical supplies and doctors and nurses to disaster areas. They take sick and injured people to hospital.

▽ An Emergency Medical Service helicopter. These helicopters, or flying ambulances, are specially equipped for carrying people to hospital in an emergency.

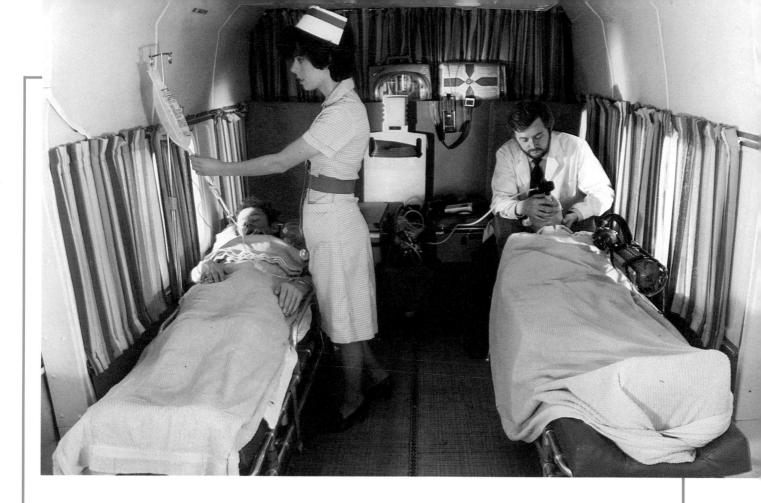

△ Inside a flying ambulance. Very sick or badly injured people can be treated and kept alive during their flight to hospital.

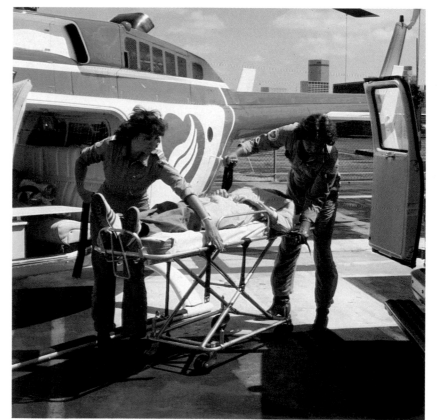

▷ A patient is transferred from a flying ambulance to a regular road ambulance.

Offshore oilfields use helicopters for many purposes. Helicopters help in the construction of drilling rigs. They provide a "bus" service for workers between their home base and the drilling platforms. They are also used for bringing in supplies and equipment for use on the platforms.

△ A helicopter waits on the helipad of an oil platform.

▽ A worker is winched off an oil rig tender. In choppy seas, even these tough little supply boats might find it dangerous to get too close to the drilling platform.

△ A helicopter with a special rig for spraying chemicals to kill pests or help crops grow.

▽ A coastguard helicopter demonstrates a rescue operation.

# Fighting helicopters

Helicopters play an important part in warfare. They are used in support of troops and for carrying equipment.

They are also deadly fighting aircraft, used by both sea and land forces. Equipped with guns and missiles, they attack enemy ships, submarines and tanks.

▽ US marines charge out of a Boeing Vertol Sea Knight, a naval version of the Boeing Vertol. These helicopters can carry up to 24 troops or 5 tonnes of vehicles and equipment. They are also used in rescue operations and can be fitted with stretchers.

▷ A Lynx III equipped with guns and rockets. These are all-purpose helicopters, used for naval warfare and in the battlefield.

▽ A Lynx firing Sura anti-tank rockets.

△ A navy helicopter comes in to land on the deck of an aircraft carrier. At sea, helicopters play an important role in anti-submarine warfare.

▽ A Sikorsky SAR (Search and Rescue) helicopter. The armed forces use helicopters for rescue operations both at sea and on land.

# Facts

## Fastest
Helicopters are not fast compared with planes, but some can reach speeds of over 350 km/h (220 mph). A speed record was set in 1986 with a specially prepared Westland Lynx. On a set course, it averaged 400 km/h (249 mph).

△ Pilot Trevor Eggington flies a Westland Lynx at a record speed over Somerset, England, in 1986.

## Largest
The biggest helicopter that has been built is the Soviet Mil 12. Its rotor tips span 67 m (220 ft), about the width of an average soccer pitch, and it weighs over 100 tonnes.

## Highest flight
A record altitude (height) for helicopters was set by an Aérospatiale Lama in 1972. It reached a height of over 12 km (7½ miles).

## Landing on water
Helicopters may be fitted with flotation bags to prevent them sinking if they have to make an emergency landing in the sea. These are fitted on the skids. Before touching down, the pilot presses a switch to release the bags and fill them with air. This keeps the helicopter afloat while the passengers and crew get out safely.

△ A Jet Ranger helicopter with floats (one on each skid) in operation on the water.

## Tilting rotors

Craft have been designed with rotors that tilt forward to act as propellers in forward flight. The result is a flying machine with the lifting power of a helicopter and the speed and range of a plane. Many of these advanced craft are now on order.

△ Inventor Kenneth Wallis waves from his autogyro, which is fitted with model missiles and has been used in a James Bond film. Wing Commander Wallis has designed and built several autogyros and has set many speed records in them.

△ The experimental Bell 301 tilt-rotor craft with its rotors beginning to tilt forward for use as propellers in forward flight.

## Flying for fun

The autogyro is a curious machine flown for fun. Its engine drives propellers, but it has no wings. It has a rotor on top which turns by itself and helps the craft to lift off the ground after just a short run.

## The first helicopters

Helicopter flight was invented in 1907, four years after the Wright brothers made the first successful aeroplane flight. A Frenchman, Paul Cornu, built a a machine with two rotors, and managed to fly it just 2 m (6 ft) straight up off the ground.

But it was another 30 years before the first successful helicopter was built. A German inventor, Henrich Focke, designed a machine with two main rotors. In 1937, he flew it for more than an hour.

# Glossary

**Autogyro**
A small, wingless machine that uses a rotor to help it get off the ground.

**Cockpit**
The cabin where the pilot sits and where the controls and instruments are.

**Co-pilot**
A qualified pilot who sits at a second set of controls and assists or relieves the pilot.

**Feeder transport**
Helicopters or small planes that take people to airports on the main air routes.

**Flotation bags**
Bags that can be filled with air and act as floats if the helicopter is forced to land on water.

**Flying crane**
A helicopter designed for lifting heavy loads.

**Helipad**
A flat platform or area on the ground, often marked with an H, for a helicopter to land on.

**Heliport**
An airport or station for helicopters.

**Rotor**
The spinning wings, or blades, of a helicopter.

**Skids**
Landing gear that looks like skis. Skids are used for landing on rough or sloping ground.

**Tail rotor**
A small rotor at the back, which balances the turning force of the main rotor and keeps the helicopter from spinning.

**Tilt-rotor**
A rotor that tilts forward to act as a propeller in forward flight.

**Winch**
A device for lifting or lowering people or things.

# Index

aircraft carrier 25
airport 14
altitude 26
ambulance 19
autogyro 27, 28

baggage 12
Bell-301 27
Boeing Vertol 11, 12, 13, 23
"bus" service 20

cargo 12
carrying 12, 14, 23
Chinook 11, 13
coastguard 18, 22
cockpit 9, 28
controls 8, 9
co-pilot 9, 28

feeder transport 14, 28
fighting helicopters 23, 24, 25
fire-fighting 16, 17
firemen 17
flotation bags 26, 28
flying a helicopter 8
flying ambulance 18, 19
flying crane 12, 13, 28

helipad 20, 28
heliport 7, 14, 28
hover 6, 7, 8

Jet Ranger 26

Lama 26
landing wheels 11
lifting 7, 10, 12

Lynx III 24

medical service 18
Mil-12 26

oil rig 14, 20

passengers 14, 15, 26
pilot 8, 9
police 16
propellers 27
Puma 10

rescue 7, 16, 17, 18, 22, 23, 25
rotor 6, 10, 11, 26, 27, 28
runway 6

Sea Knight 23
search 16, 18, 25
Sikorsky 25
skids 11, 26, 28
speed 26
spraying 22

tail 10, 28
tilt-rotor 27, 28
troops 23

warfare 23
Westland Lynx 26
winch 17, 18, 21, 28
wings 6, 27